Let’s Go Fisl

我们去钓鱼

wǒ men qù diào yú

Written by Dr. Qixia Yu
Edited by Jerry Gao
Illustrated by Hiruni Kariyawasam

Love
FISHING
DIARY

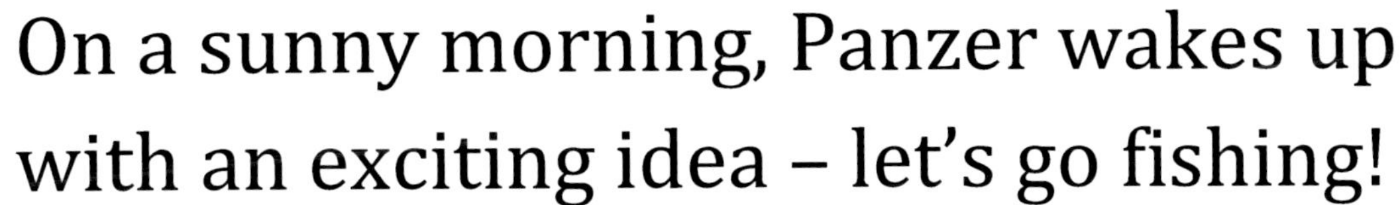
On a sunny morning, Panzer wakes up with an exciting idea – let’s go fishing!

yī gè qíng lǎng de zǎo chén, Panzer yī jué xǐng lái,
一个晴朗的早晨，Panzer一觉醒来，
tú rán mào chū yī gè hǎo zhǔ yì – wǒ men qù diào yú!
突然冒出一个好主意 – 我们去钓鱼！

“Fishing is a family tradition, and I can also enjoy the beautiful view while I’m there! ”
she exclaims, rushing to her twin sister, Noodle.

“diào yú shì wǒ men jiā de chuán tǒng,
“钓鱼是我们家的传统，

ér qiě wǒ hái kě yǐ xīn shǎng měi lì de fēng jǐng!”
而且我还可以欣赏美丽的风景！”

tā zì yán zì yǔ, jí cōng cōng de bēn xiàng mèi mei Noodle。
她自言自语，急匆匆地奔向妹妹Noodle。

“Wakey-wakey, it’s time to go fishing!” Panzer purrs to Noodle.

“xǐng xǐng, xǐng xǐng, wǒ men qù diào yú!”
“醒醒，醒醒，我们去钓鱼!”
Panzer duì zhe Noodle gū lū jiào zhe。
Panzer对着Noodle咕噜叫着。

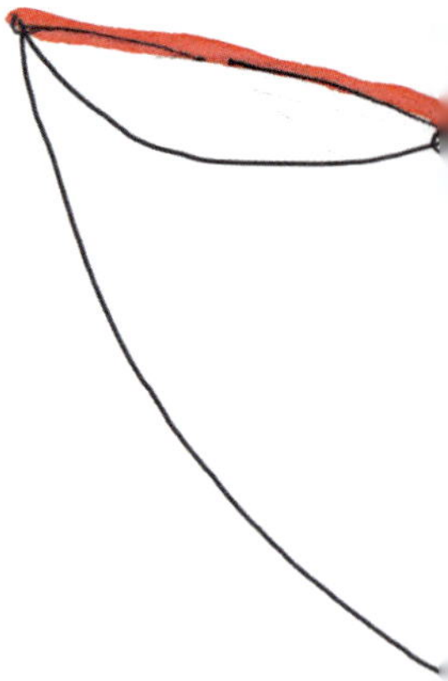

Then, Panzer begins to pack up her fishing gear, hastily tossing the fishing rod, reel, and float into a bucket.

rán hòu,   Panzer jiù qù shōu shí tā de diào yú gōng jù,
然后, Panzer 就去收拾她的钓鱼工具,
tā bǎ diào yú gān、diào yú xiàn hé fú piāo
她把钓鱼竿、钓鱼线和浮漂
dōu yī gǔ nǎo de rēng jìn le tǒng lǐ。
都一股脑地扔进了桶里。

P

They head to the Golden Ear River,
where there are all kinds of fish –
salmon, trout, and many more.

tā men lái dào le jīn ěr duǒ hé,
她们来到了金耳朵河,
zhè lǐ yǒu gè zhǒng gè yàn de yú –
这里有各种各样的鱼 –
sān wèn yú 、zūn yú hé hěn duō jiào bù shàng míng zì de yú。
三文鱼、鳟鱼和很多叫不上名字的鱼。

Settled on the upper riverbank, they have a perfect view of the flowing river and all the marvelous fish swimming beneath the water. What a gorgeous sight!

lái dào hé liú de shàng yóu, tā men zài zhè lǐ
来到河流的上游，她们在这里
kě yǐ kàn dào xiǎo hé liú shuǐ hé lái huí yóu dòng de yú er,
可以看到小河流水和来回游动的鱼儿，
duō me měi lì de jǐng sè!
多么美丽的景色！

They wait patiently for a harvest.
Soon, Panzer's bucket becomes
a treasure trove of fish,
including her favorite – a big salmon.

rán hòu, tā men nài xīn děng dài zhuó dà fēng shōu。
然后，她们耐心等待着大丰收。
hěn kuài, Panzer de tǒng lǐ zhuāng mǎn le gè zhǒng gè yàng de yú,
很快，Panzer的桶里装满了各种各样的鱼，
hái yǒu yī tiáo tā zuì ài chī de sān wèn yú。
还有一条她最爱吃的三文鱼。

“Wow, not a bad haul!” exclaims an amazed Noodle.
“It’s nothing,” says Panzer, though she is happy to hear Noodle’s compliment.
What a humble cat!

“ wa, shōu huò bù xiǎo a!” Noodle gǎn tàn dào。
“哇, 收获不小啊!” Noodle感叹道。
“zhè méi shén me,” Panzer huí dá,
“这没什么,” Panzer回答，
jǐn guǎn tā tīng dào Noodle de kuā jiǎng hěn gāo xìng。
尽管她听到Noodle的夸奖很高兴。
duō me qiān xū de Panzer!
多么谦虚的Panzer!

“jīn tiān wǎn shàng jiù chī sān wèn yú ba,”
“今天晚上就吃三文鱼吧,”
Panzer zhèng zài jì huà wǎn cān。
Panzer正在计划晚餐。
tā yào kǎo yú、 zhà yú、 hái shì zuò shēng yú piàn ne?
她要烤鱼、炸鱼、还是做生鱼片呢？

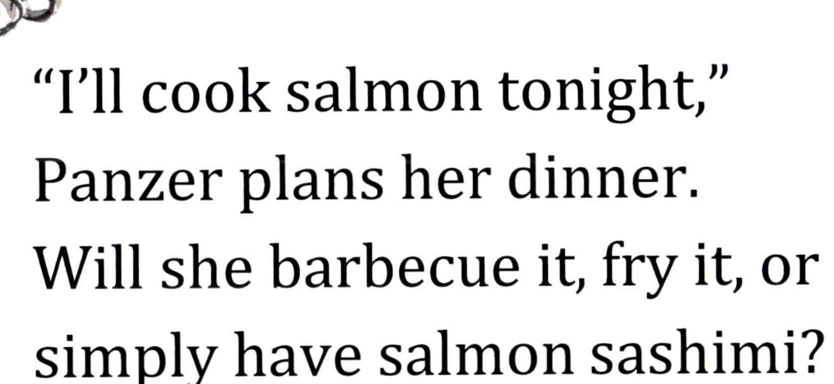

"I'll cook salmon tonight,"
Panzer plans her dinner.
Will she barbecue it, fry it, or
simply have salmon sashimi?

However, her joy takes a sudden dip
when she notices her salmon has disappeared.

rán ér,　tā de kuài lè hěn kuài shòu dào le dǎ jí,
然而，她的快乐很快受到了打击，
yīn wèi tā de sān wèn yú bù jiàn le。
因为她的三文鱼不见了。

P
N

“Where did it go?” Panzer wonders. “Maybe it jumped out of the bucket?” Noodle looks around.

Panzer: “tā qù nǎ er le?”

Panzer: “它去哪儿了?”

Noodle: “huì bù huì tiào le chū qù?”

Noodle: “会不会跳了出去?”

Aha! There stands Ben, the mischievous cat, gobbling up Panzer's salmon, not far away.

a hā! bù yuǎn chù, nà zhǐ tiáo pí dǎo dàn māo Ben,
啊哈！不远处，那只调皮捣蛋猫Ben，
zhèng zài láng tūn hǔ yàn de chī Panzer de sān wèn yú。
正在狼吞虎咽地吃Panzer的三文鱼。

“Hey you! That’s my salmon!
Keep your grubby paws off my fish!”
Panzer cries out furiously.

“hēi!　nà shì wǒ de sān wèn yú,
“嘿! 那是我的三文鱼，
lí wǒ de yú yuǎn diǎn!”
离我的鱼远点!”
Panzer sheng qì de hǎn dào。
Panzer生气地喊道。

P

“But your fish is so tasty. Why do I always get those slimy fish? They make me sick. Besides, other cats’ fish always taste better,” complains the chatty Ben, going on and on.

“kě shì, nǐ de yú tài hào chī le; wèi shé me wǒ zǒng shì
“可是, 你的鱼太好吃了; 为什么我总是
diào dào nián hú hú de yú? yī diǎn dōu bù hào chī,
钓到粘糊糊的鱼? 一点都不好吃,
ér qí tā māo diào de yú zǒng shì bǐ zì jǐ de hào chī?”
而其他猫钓的鱼总是比自己的好吃?”
huà láo bān de Ben bào yuàn gè bù tíng。
话痨般的Ben抱怨个不停。

“It’s rude to grab my fish without asking.
I’ve already planned a salmon dinner.
Now you’ve ruined it!” Panzer protests.

“bù qǐng zì qǔ shì hěn bù lǐ mào de,
“不请自取是很不礼貌的,
ér qiě wǒ yǐ jīng jì huà hǎo le wǎn cān chī sān wèn yú, xiàn zài kě hǎo,
而且我已经计划好了晚餐吃三文鱼, 现在可好,
sān wèn yú yǐ jīng bèi nǐ chī diào le!” Panzer hěn bù gāo xìng de shuō。
三文鱼已经被你吃掉了!” Panzer很不高兴地说。

P

Noodle: “Why not teach him how to fish?”
Panzer: “Well, the fishing skill runs in our family. I’m not sure I can pass it on to him. But I’ll try.”

Noodle: “yīng gāi jiào gěi tā rú hé diào yú?”
Noodle: “应该教给他如何钓鱼?”
Panzer: “kě shì, zhè shì zán men zǔ chuán de běn lǐng,
Panzer: “可是, 这是咱们祖传的本领,
wǒ bù què dìng néng bù néng jiào huì tā, dàn shì wǒ shì shì kàn ba。”
我不确定能不能教会他, 但是我试试看吧。”

How generous Panzer is!

duō me kāng kǎi dà fāng de Panzer!

多么慷慨大方的Panzer!

"Actually, nobody ever taught me how to fish," mumbles Ben.

"qí shí, cóng lái jiù méi rén jiào guò wǒ rú hé diào yú,"

"其实,从来就没人教过我如何钓鱼,"

Ben dū nāng zhe。

Ben嘟囔着。

Panzer starts teaching Ben immediately:
“First of all, be quiet, not so chatty! Don’t fidget!
Don’t clean your face or lick your paws!”

Panzer mǎ shàng kāi shǐ jiào tā:
Panzer马上开始教他：
“shǒu xiān, nǐ yào bǎo chí ān jìng, bù yào zuò xiǎo dòng zuò,
“首先，你要保持安静，不要做小动作，
bù yào xǐ liǎn huò zhě tiǎn zhuǎ zi。”
不要洗脸或者舔爪子。”

“Pay no attention to butterflies or dragonflies, no matter how tempting they are. Pretend you’re meditating, and a fishy feast will come to you,” Panzer continues.

“bié qù lǐ huì fēi lái de hú dié hé qīng tíng,
“别去理会飞来的蝴蝶和蜻蜓,
bù guǎn tā men duō me yòu rén;
不管它们多么诱人;
bì mù yǎng shén, nài xīn děng dài, yuàn wàng zǒng huì shí xiàn,”
闭目养神，耐心等待，愿望总会实现,”
Panzer jì xù shuō。
Panzer继续说。

Ben listens well and tries his best to follow Panzer's words. Then, he sets up his rod and meditates.

Ben xǐ ěr gōng tīng, bǎi hǎo diào yú gān hòu, jiù kāi shǐ míng sī。

Ben洗耳恭听, 摆好钓鱼竿后，就开始冥思。

A colorful butterfly flutters by; it doesn’t dazzle Ben.
A dragonfly tickles his nose; he doesn’t scratch.

yī zhī huā hú dié fēi lái,　Ben bù wéi zhī suǒ dòng。
一支花蝴蝶飞来, Ben不为之所动。
yī zhǐ qīng tíng lái náo Ben,　tā yě méi yǒu náo yǎng yang。
一只蜻蜓来挠Ben, 他也没有挠痒痒。

A huge salmon swims by, but Ben, too focused on meditation, lets the salmon slip away. What a loss!

yī tiáo dà sān wèn yú yóu guò, Ben tài jí zhōng jīng lì míng sī,
一条大三文鱼游过, Ben太集中精力冥思，
jié guǒ sān wèn yú liū zǒu le。
结果三文鱼溜走了。
tài kě xí le!
太可惜了！

Ben keeps fishing diligently.
Soon, he catches trout, catfish, and salmon.

Ben jì xù nǔ lì de chuí diào,
Ben继续努力地垂钓,
hěn kuài, tā diào dào le zūn yú、 nián yú hé sān wèn yú。
很快, 他钓到了鳟鱼、鲶鱼和三文鱼。

With joy in his whiskers and a smile on his face,
he rolls over and over in happiness.
What a superb fisher he is!

Ben xǐ bù zì jīn, gāo xìng de zài dì shàng dǎ gǔn,
Ben喜不自禁，高兴地在地上打滚，
duō me chū sè de diào yú gāo shǒu。
多么出色的钓鱼高手。

However, trouble is not far behind;
the sly Cici is approaching the buckets.

rán ér, má fan hěn kuài jiù lái le,
然而, 麻烦很快就来了,
nà zhī jiǎo huá de māo Cici qiāo qiāo de kào jìn le yú tǒng。
那只狡猾的猫Cici 悄悄地靠近了鱼桶。

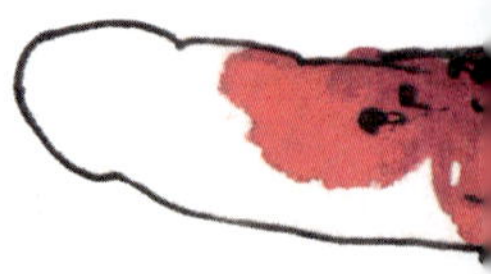

“Oh my, oh my!” she meows as her paw reaches for the bucket. So, when Ben drops another fish in, he finds all the buckets empty.

tā miāo miāo jiào zhe, zhuǎ zi shēn xiàng yú tǒng;
她喵喵叫着， 爪子伸向鱼桶;
dāng Ben yòu diào dào yī tiáo yú shí,
当Ben又钓到一条鱼时,
tā fā xiàn yú tǒng yǐ jīng kōng dàng dàng le。
他发现鱼桶已经空荡荡了。

Acknowledgement

Elizabeth Alexander-Cook

Hiruni Kariyawasam

Jerry Gao

Megan Polstra

Contact: QX.Living@gmail.com

Made in the USA
Las Vegas, NV
01 December 2024